Cambridge Discovery Education™
▶ INTERACTIVE READERS

Series editor: Bob Hastings

GOLD
GREED AND GLORY

Brian Sargent

CAMBRIDGE UNIVERSITY PRESS

Discovery EDUCATION

CAMBRIDGE UNIVERSITY PRESS
Cambridge, New York, Melbourne, Madrid, Cape Town,
Singapore, São Paulo, Delhi, Mexico City

Cambridge University Press
32 Avenue of the Americas, New York, NY 10013-2473, USA

www.cambridge.org
Information on this title: www.cambridge.org/9781107652606

© Cambridge University Press 2014

This publication is in copyright. Subject to statutory exception and to the provisions of relevant collective licensing agreements, no reproduction of any part may take place without the written permission of Cambridge University Press.

First published 2014

Printed in Hong Kong, China, by Golden Cup Printing Company Limited

A catalog record for this publication is available from the British Library.

Library of Congress Cataloging-in-Publication Data

Sargent, Brian, 1969-
 Gold : greed and glory : level B1 / Brian Sargent.
   pages cm. -- (Cambridge discovery interactive readers)
 ISBN 978-1-107-65260-6 (pbk. : alk. paper)
 1. Gold--Juvenile literature. 2. Readers (Elementary) 3. English language--Textbooks for foreign speakers. I. Title.

TN761.6.S37 2014
669'.22--dc23

2013014266

ISBN 978-1-107-65260-6

Additional resources for this publication at www.cambridge.org
Cambridge University Press has no responsibility for the persistence or accuracy of URLs for external or third-party Internet Web sites referred to in this publication and does not guarantee that any content on such Web sites is, or will remain, accurate or appropriate.

Layout services, art direction, book design, and photo research: Q2ABillSMITH GROUP
Editorial services: Hyphen S.A.
Audio production: CityVox, New York
Video production: Q2ABillSMITH GROUP

Contents

Before You Read: Get Ready! 4

CHAPTER 1
The Importance of Gold 6

CHAPTER 2
The Dark History of Gold 10

CHAPTER 3
The Gold Rush 14

CHAPTER 4
The Past and Future of Gold 20

CHAPTER 5
What Do You Think? 24

After You Read 26

Answer Key 28

Glossary

Before You Read: Get Ready!

Words to Know

Complete the sentences with the correct words.

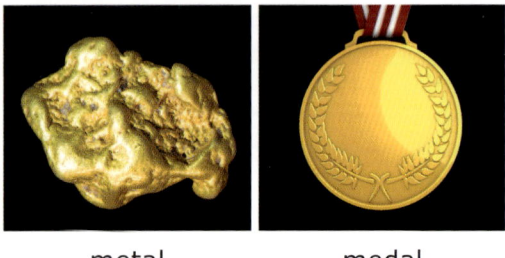

metal   medal

❶ A winner of a race can earn a _____.
❷ The bridge is made of _____.

Words to Know

Read the paragraph. Then complete the definitions with the correct highlighted words.

Gold is very rare. For thousands of years, people have looked for it. Explorers traveled the world to find gold. Gold is often made into jewelry, but today it can also be found in unexpected places. It is in our computers and other electronic goods. It is even in space! Gold is a soft metal, and it melts at just 1,064° Celsius. This means gold is easy to work with.

❶ _____: things for sale or to own
❷ _____: very unusual
❸ _____: becomes soft and easy to pour when it is heated
❹ _____: people who discover new places

Words to Know

Read the paragraph. Then complete the definitions with the correct highlighted words.

In 1848, many Americans moved west to look for gold in California. They traveled in wagons. The travelers often got sick or sometimes were attacked by native people during the long, dangerous journey. Some prospectors looked for gold in the rivers, and others dug big holes under the ground. Inside these big holes, miners looked for gold for many hours every day.

❶ _____ : people looking for gold

❷ _____ : people who look underground for gold or other valuable things

❸ _____ : people travel in these; they are pulled by horses

❹ _____ : people who lived in an area first

CHAPTER 1

The Importance of Gold

GOLD SHOWS IMPORTANCE. PEOPLE USE IT IN ART AND IN MONEY. THEY USE IT IN RELIGION AND IN JEWELRY.

Olympic Gold

Constantina Dita from Romania made history at the 2008 Beijing Olympics. At 38 years old, she ran over 42 kilometers in two hours, 26 minutes, and 44 seconds. She became the world's oldest Olympic marathon[1] winner. She won a gold medal.

Constantina was not alone. Hundreds of athletes win gold medals at sports competitions. Their gold medals show they are the strongest, the fastest, and the best athletes in the world. Gold is rare and special. A gold medal means "I'm number one."

[1] **marathon:** a race in which people run for 42.195 kilometers

What is gold?

Gold is a metal, like silver. Gold, however, is different from most metals because gold does not corrode.

Ancient silver   Ancient gold

Corroding is when the metal is slowly destroyed. Time, air, and water corrode most metals. Compare these two coins. One is ancient silver. It appears **dull** or dirty. The ancient gold coin shines like new.

Gold is heavy. Pure gold weighs 19.3 times more than water. Imagine a ball of gold the size of a basketball. It would weigh 144 kilograms!

At 1,064° Celsius, gold melts. Melted gold can be made into many different shapes, and these shapes can be melted again into new shapes. Nothing is lost when gold is melted. Gold can be used over and over again. Much of the gold we have today used to be something else. Perhaps the gold in Constantina's Olympic medal used to be in a king's crown.[2]

[2] **crown:** what a king or a queen wears on his or her head

There is very little gold in the world. Throughout history people have discovered approximately 165 metric tonnes of gold. That is the size of a small office building!

Beautiful Gold

Gold has many uses. The color and shine of gold make it perfect for art. And gold is soft. You can cut pure gold with a knife.

Imagine hitting pure gold with a hammer.[3] The gold becomes thinner, but does not lose its shine. If you continue hitting the gold, it becomes thinner and thinner. Soon, a small piece of gold can become a large, flat sheet – like paper. This flat sheet of gold is called gold leaf.

Ancient Egyptians were expert gold workers. They often used gold leaf in their art. They liked to put a thin cover of gold on statues and objects.[4] This is called gilding. Many say Ancient Egypt's gilded art is still the best in the world.

[3] **hammer:** something with a heavy metal piece at one end, used to hit things
[4] **object:** a thing you can see or touch but is not alive

A gilded Egyptian head

Gold jewelry

Today, gilding with gold is very common. In fact, Olympic gold medals are no longer made of pure gold. They are made of silver! In 1920, they decided to make the medals of silver and then gild them with gold.

Because gold is soft, it is perfect for gilding; however, it is bad for jewelry making. Imagine a soft ring! It would change its shape. And a beautiful soft necklace would break! The Ancient Egyptians knew what to do. They mixed the gold with other metals. This made the gold stronger. A mix of metals is called an alloy.

Today gold alloys are much more common than pure gold. Almost all modern gold jewelry is an alloy. This makes the jewelry stronger. It also allows a small amount of gold to be used in many different pieces. This makes the jewelry less expensive.

EVALUATE

There are many metals more rare than gold. Why do you think gold is so important?

CHAPTER 2

The Dark History of Gold

FOR 6,000 YEARS, PEOPLE HAVE COLLECTED AND USED GOLD. MANY PEOPLE HAVE DIED WHILE LOOKING FOR IT, OR TAKING IT FROM OTHERS.

Statue of Francisco Vázquez de Coronado

Looking for Gold

Gold can be very tiny pieces, like a powder, or it can be a small rock called a nugget. It can be found anywhere, but some areas have more gold than others. South Africa, Canada, the United States, Russia, China, Brazil, and Australia all have large amounts of gold.

Even today, people find gold in these places. In 2008, a boy in California, USA, went fishing with his father. Instead of fish, he found 170 grams of gold in the lake. It was worth $5,500. He was very lucky. Some people in history, however, were not so lucky.

Coronado and the Cities of Gold

In 1540, a Spanish explorer named Francisco Vázquez de Coronado was not just looking for a gold nugget in a lake. He was looking for a golden city. Coronado was a conquistador.

Conquistadors were Spanish or Portuguese explorers and soldiers who came to the Americas looking for land, adventure, and gold. Coronado had heard a story about a place called Cibola. The story said Cibola had seven cities made of gold.

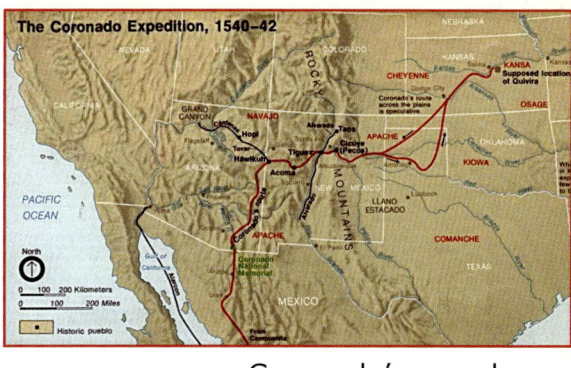

Coronado's search for Cibola

Excitement for gold made many Europeans come to the Americas. When the conquistadors arrived, they met many native people. The Europeans killed many of them for their gold. Other times, they enslaved[5] the native people and made them dig for the gold. They stole the native people's land and other valuable things.

Coronado formed a group of more than 300 soldiers and about 1,000 Indians. Together, they looked for Cibola. Many people died while they were looking, and Coronado's men fought many battles. Of course, Coronado never found a golden city. Instead, he learned Cibola was just an ordinary village.

[5] **enslave:** control a person or a group of people by keeping them in a situation where they are not free

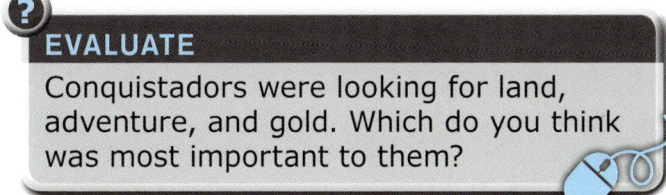

EVALUATE

Conquistadors were looking for land, adventure, and gold. Which do you think was most important to them?

Pizarro and the Sun King

European greed[6] for gold changed the Americas forever. Conquistadors and other European explorers did terrible things to native people so that they could get gold to take home.

In the 1500s, there were 12 million Incas living in South America. These native people called themselves the Children of the Sun. They believed the sun was a god and that gold was his sweat.[7] Their land had an incredible amount of gold. The Incas used it in many ways. They made it into statues, jewelry, cups, and spoons. Even the water pipes in the king's palace were made of gold.

Then news of their gold came to the conquistadors.

---

[6]**greed:** when you want more than you need
[7]**sweat:** your skin makes this when your body is too hot

Atahualpa and Pizarro

In 1532, a Spaniard named Francisco Pizarro arrived in the land of the Children of the Sun. He brought a small army, less than 200 men. Pizarro invited Atahualpa, the Sun King, to a meeting. He said he wanted to have a peaceful meeting. When Atahualpa appeared, however, Pizarro broke his promise. He and his men attacked.

Thousands of Incas died in the fighting. Pizarro locked the Sun King away. He made another promise to the Incas. If they gave him a room full of gold, he would return Atahualpa. The Incas did what Pizarro asked. They filled a room with gold and waited for Pizarro to send Atahualpa home. Instead, Pizarro broke his promise again. He murdered the Sun King and took the Incas' gold.

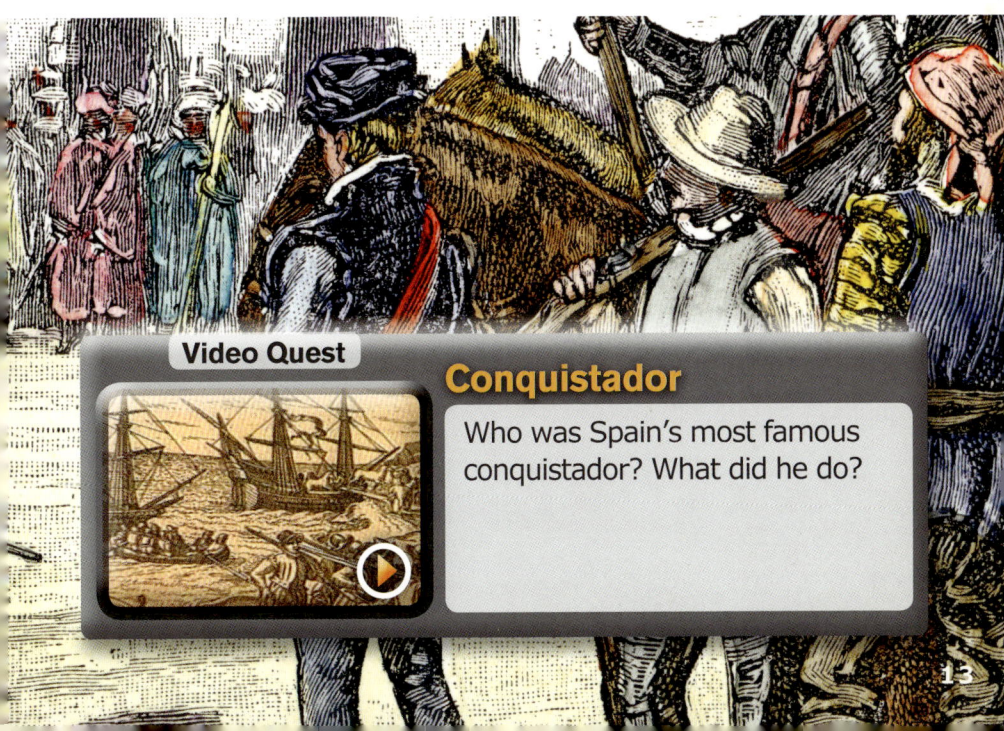

Video Quest

Conquistador

Who was Spain's most famous conquistador? What did he do?

CHAPTER 3

The Gold Rush

IN 1848, PEOPLE IN THE UNITED STATES HEARD ABOUT GOLD IN CALIFORNIA. MANY OF THEM LEFT THEIR HOMES AND THEIR FAMILIES AND MOVED WEST.

John Sutter lived in California, USA. He owned a sawmill, a factory that cuts trees for wood. On January 24, 1848, his partner, James Marshall, found a small piece of gold in the river near the sawmill. Sutter and Marshall did not tell anyone about the gold. They wanted it to be a secret. Sutter did not want crowds of people moving to Sutter's Mill.

However, workers from the sawmill learned about the gold. They went to the river and looked around. They found more gold, and soon the secret was out. News of the gold traveled all around California. In only eight months, more than 4,000 **prospectors** moved to the hills near Sutter's Mill.

The gold **rush** had begun.

At the beginning of 1848, San Francisco was a busy town. By that summer, it was nearly empty. Almost everyone had gone. Doctors, lawyers, soldiers, bankers, store owners, even the mayor[8] left the city, looking for gold. The people who stayed in San Francisco looked for gold, too. They dug up the streets of the town hoping to find tiny pieces of gold there.

A few of the first prospectors in California became rich. There was a lot of gold in the area. A lucky prospector could earn over $300 a day. **Miners** built camps across the state, and those camps quickly became small towns. California was catching **gold fever**.

[8] **mayor:** the leader of a town

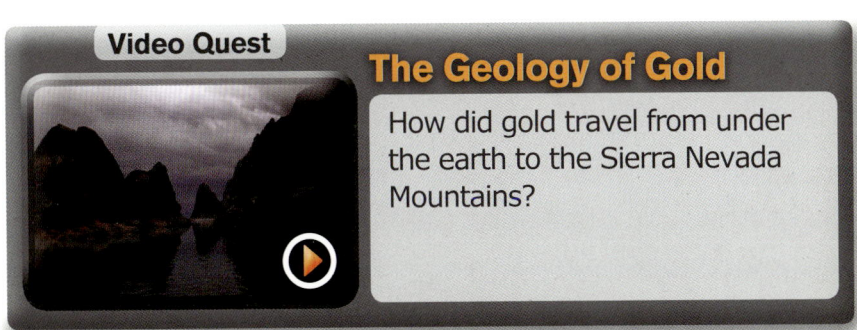

Video Quest

The Geology of Gold

How did gold travel from under the earth to the Sierra Nevada Mountains?

Prospecting for gold

Gold Fever

On December 5, 1848, US President James Polk gave a speech. He announced that there was gold in California. He said the amount was "very large."

Thousands of people caught gold fever. They left their homes to travel to California. Many did not arrive. Some made the dangerous trip by sea, around the bottom of South America. Many of the ships sank on the journey. Others traveled the width of the country in wagons pulled by horses. They faced[9] many dangers, including illness, bad weather, and attacks by native people.

Despite the danger, about 90,000 miners and prospectors successfully arrived in California. The year was 1849, so these people were called forty-niners. They had dreams of becoming rich. Sadly, their dreams did not come true. There was not as much gold in California as everyone thought. In the end, most forty-niners found very little gold.

[9]**face:** deal with something difficult or unpleasant

The forty-niners lived in camps and slept in tents. When a man found some gold, he had to be careful. Stealing was common. The camps were dirty, and illness was a big problem. Life was hard.

A long, hard day of work could bring a lucky prospector one ounce (about 28 grams) of gold. In 1849, one ounce of gold was worth $16. This was not a lot of money for a prospector. Food was very expensive. A breakfast in San Francisco could cost over $20. A shovel[10] cost $36. In the end, very few prospectors became rich.

The Richest Man in California

One man did become very rich. He was a businessman, not a prospector. His name was Sam Brannan, and he owned several California newspapers. He also owned a small store at Sutter's Mill. When gold was discovered there, Brannan wrote about it in his newspapers. When prospectors arrived, they bought things at his store. Brannan became very successful. He became California's first **millionaire**.

Samuel Brannan

[10]**shovel:** something used for digging

Video Quest

Gold Rush

Why did the US build a railroad connecting the East to the West?

Native Americans and the Gold Rush

Before 1849, about 150,000 Native Americans lived in California. Many of them became prospectors during the gold rush. However, life was different for Native American prospectors. Often, their gold and land were stolen. Native Americans' gold was weighed differently. It was called an Indian ounce, and Native Americans were paid only half the price of a normal ounce.

A man named James Savage used Native Americans as workers. He collected gold from his workers and paid them the same weight in other things.

For example, he gave the Native Americans a three-pound (1.4 kilogram) blanket for three pounds of gold. There were many people like Savage in California.

In 1850, Californians made a new law. It did not help Native Americans, especially the children. It said bosses must give Native American child workers food and clothes. That was all. If they did not, the bosses had to pay the government just $10. This law was repealed, or stopped, in 1863.

CHAPTER 4

The Past and Future of Gold

YOU PROBABLY USE THINGS WITH GOLD IN THEM EVERY DAY. SOME OF THE USES MAY SURPRISE YOU.

Useful Gold

Surprisingly, few ancient cultures used gold for money. Many believe the Lydians were the first to do this. Lydia was a Middle Eastern city-state and, in the 7th century BCE, they invented gold coins.

After Lydia, gold coins also appeared in Ancient Greece. Greek coins quickly became very popular. Many have been discovered in faraway places, such as India, China, and Northern Europe.

Besides using gold coins, the Greeks also invented a way to weigh gold. They used the seeds[11] of a tree called a carob tree. The Greeks decided that one gold coin should weigh the same as 24 carob seeds.

Carob seeds

[11] **seed:** a small round thing that a new plant can grow from

20

Gold used in electronics

Today, gold is **measured** in *karats,* from the Greek "carob." Karats are used to measure the purity of gold. For example, 24-karat gold is pure gold, and 12-karat gold is an alloy – half gold, half other metals.

Gold money was very useful. Its use led to modern banking. However, another modern use may be more important. Gold is a metal. Like most metals, it conducts electricity. That means electricity can travel through it easily. Gold is special because it conducts electricity better than most other metals. Even a small amount of gold can conduct electricity.

Gold is the perfect metal for electronic goods. Because it conducts electricity well and does not corrode, it does not need to be replaced[12] often. Computer parts are often made of gold. It is also used in our phones and calculators.[13] Almost everything small and electronic uses some gold.

[12] **replace:** get something new because the one you had before has been lost or damaged
[13] **calculator:** a small machine that you use to do math

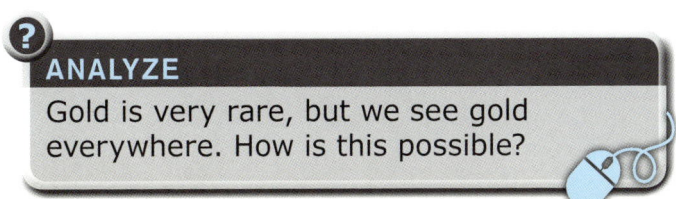

ANALYZE
Gold is very rare, but we see gold everywhere. How is this possible?

Gold in Medicine

In 16th-century France, a woman named Diane de Poitiers drank gold. She was not alone. Drinking gold was popular then. People drank gold to stay young and beautiful. Of course, it did not work. Drinking a lot of gold is not good for you. For Diane de Poitiers, drinking gold killed her.

Drinking gold does not make you young or beautiful. However, some kinds of gold have been used in medicine for many years. In fact, some doctors are now using gold to help cancer[14] patients. Doctors use tiny pieces of gold together with special medicines. The gold helps the medicine find the patients' problem areas and use the medicine in the best way.

[14] **cancer:** a serious illness

Gold is Everywhere

Even though there is very little gold in the world, we see it everywhere. There is gold in jewelry and art. We use gold in computers and cell phones. We use gold in medicine and hospitals. We send gold into space. Gold from the Earth has traveled to the moon and even to Mars.

More gold is found every year, and people are finding more uses for gold as well. Who knows what the future of gold will be?

Gold is used to protect astronauts from the brightness and heat of the sun.

CHAPTER 5

What Do You Think?

Gold of the Incas in Your Phone?

When Francisco Pizarro attacked the Incan people, he also destroyed their **treasures**. Before sending their gold back to Spain, he melted it. He turned it into small pieces, called ingots. Because of Pizarro, we will never know much about the art and beauty of Incan gold.

In Spain, the gold was melted again. It became new things. Since then, some of those things have probably been melted again and again.

Do you have any gold jewelry? Do you wear a gold ring or necklace? Do you think it could be gold of the Incas? If so, how do you feel about that?

Do you have a cell phone? Do you have a computer? There is likely gold inside those things. If they had Incan gold, how would you feel?

The Gold Standard

When paper money was invented, it was often with a gold standard. That meant the paper money was worth a certain amount of gold. Under the gold standard, you could go to a bank, give them your paper money, and ask for gold. If someone owed you money, you could insist on gold instead.

In 1933, the United States stopped using the gold standard. Too many people were asking for gold and keeping it. There was not enough money for the country. Today, no country in the world uses the gold standard for their paper money.

Would you like to return to the gold standard? Would you like to use gold for money?

The gold standard written on paper money

After You Read

True or False

Read the sentences and choose Ⓐ (True) or Ⓑ (False).

1 Gold keeps its shine over time.
   Ⓐ True
   Ⓑ False

2 Gold is a hard metal.
   Ⓐ True
   Ⓑ False

3 Conquistadors were cruel to native peoples.
   Ⓐ True
   Ⓑ False

4 Pizarro wanted to become friends with the Incan king.
   Ⓐ True
   Ⓑ False

5 Most prospectors in California found very little gold.
   Ⓐ True
   Ⓑ False

6 Most metals conduct electricity better than gold.
   Ⓐ True
   Ⓑ False

7 Gold is very useful in electronic goods.
   Ⓐ True
   Ⓑ False

Answer the Questions

Answer the questions in your own words. Use information that you learned from this reader.

1 What often happened when native peoples met with conquistadors?

_____

_____

_____

2 Describe the life of a prospector during California's gold rush.

_____

_____

_____

3 Why is gold important in today's electronics?

_____

_____

_____

Complete the Text

Use the words in the box to complete the paragraph.

| forty-niners | gold | nuggets | powder | rich |

When **1** _____ was found in California, many people traveled there. They were called **2** _____. They lived in camps. Lucky prospectors found large gold **3** _____, but most found only gold **4** _____. Many prospectors returned home without becoming **5** _____.

27

Answer Key

Words to Know, page 4
① medal ② metal

Words to Know, page 4
① goods ② rare ③ melts ④ explorers

Words to Know, page 5
① prospectors ② miners ③ wagons ④ native people

Evaluate, page 9 *Answers will vary.*

Evaluate, page 11 *Answers will vary.*

Video Quest, page 13
Hernán Cortés attacked the Aztec ruler Montezuma. He stole the Aztecs' treasures and destroyed their city.

Video Quest, page 15
Suggested Answer: Volcanoes carried the gold from deep under the ground inside super hot water. When the water cooled, the gold cooled, and it stayed all over the mountains.

Video Quest, page 17
Suggested Answer: During the gold rush, many people moved to the western part of the United States. After the gold rush, the railroad helped people travel back and forth.

Analyze, page 21 *Answers will vary.*

True or False, page 26
① A ② B ③ A ④ B ⑤ A ⑥ B ⑦ A

Answer the questions, page 27 *Answers will vary.*

Complete the Text, page 27
① gold ② forty-niners ③ nuggets ④ powder ⑤ rich